Speed Hypnosis

By

Anthony Taylor

Copyright

Authors note

The information contained within these pages is for entertainment only. The author makes no claims that any part of the information is intended to be educational.

Practicing any of the guidance contained herein is at the users discretion and risk.

You are advised to take proper training courses and become qualified before attempting to use any skills mentioned in this book.

That having been said, have fun and practice safe hypnosis look after yourself and those for whom you make yourself responsible.

What is hypnosis

This is one of the most common questions any hypnotist will be asked. As with all things hypnosis there is more than one school of thought. There are lots of opinions about what exactly hypnosis is here are the most common.

A highly relaxed and receptive state of mind.

An altered state of consciousness

A splitting of the conscious and unconscious mind

A form of waking sleep

A meditative state.

So you see there is no one answer to the question what is hypnosis. One thing in which all of us are in agreement is that it is a natural state which all humans are capable of achieving.

Another school of thought takes a completely opposite view. They say it does not exist at all and that hypnotised people simply play along with the hypnotist, just like game show contestants play along with ridiculous suggestions of the host.

For the purposes of this book, I think the best description is that hypnosis is a state of mind where the hypnotised person may respond more favourably to suggestions than in a normal waking state, regardless of the technical reasons.

That is not to say that they are zombies complying mindlessly with whatever a hypnotists says, it means that they may be more receptive to positive verbal input.

In fact negative suggestion will be either rejected or modified to suit the hypnotee.

Having looked at what hypnosis is it's worth just saying here what hypnosis isn't.

Its not mind control even someone acting like an idiot on stage knows what he is doing. the hypnotist is not 'in control' of the hypnotee. this myth is generated by film and TV for entertainment reasons only.

Its not dangerous in and of itself. Any dangers that may be present during hypnosis will be physical dangers. slip trip hazards and the like. There are absolutely no psychological dangers.

It's not voodoo or any other kind of magic.

It's not unnatural. Cultures around the world use meditation and self hypnosis in all sorts of ways for all sorts of reasons. In fact we in the west used to use it. We have over the centuries simply lost the ability through lack of use.

Another really common question is, 'What does it feel like to be hypnotised?'

First the question should be modified to 'what does it feel like to be in a trance'.

This is a very difficult question to answer directly since everyone experiences hypnosis in a different way. Because it is such a personal experience this is quite understandable.

The overriding feedback from hypnotees is that it is very much like the feeling they have when daydreaming or are totally engrossed in a television programme. They describe it as being similar to that moment just as you drop off to sleep at night.

Alex described hypnosis in this way.

" *You know when you are watching a film on TV, and you become so engrossed that it's like you are completely zoned in to what's happening on the screen and at the same time you are sort of zoned out of your surroundings, as if you were almost an actor on the screen. So that when your wife offers you a cup of tea you answer her automatically, without realising you have. Well that's what being hypnotised was like for me.*"

Paul had a completely different experience.

"It was great, as if nothing really mattered. I felt like I was just floating in this worry free place almost as if I was on a light fluffy cloud, and that a friendly voice was speaking good sense to me, and I knew it was good sense because I already knew what was being said. The voice just confirmed things for me. I haven't smoked a cigarette since."

The common thread is that the experience is really good. That the hypnotee feels the best they have ever felt. They wake up feeling refreshed and confident, and apparently when they go home they have the best night sleep of their lives.

What is speed hypnosis

So now that we have a good understanding of the basics of what hypnosis is we can look at what speed hypnosis is.

Speed hypnosis is the art of getting someone into a highly suggestible state, or into a hypnotic state, in minutes or seconds, or even instantaneously!

This is why it is sometimes called rapid or instant hypnosis. Unlike regular hypnosis we do not gently and gradually put a person into a relaxed state. Instead we send them into trance by using confusion or shock.

Speed hypnosis is used in two fundamental ways

Overtly

Covertly

Overt means that the person is aware that they are going to be hypnotised and then the hypnotist proceeds to send them into a trance very quickly. The expectation on their part is a helpful thing, they are agreeing to cooperate.

Covert hypnosis is when the person to be hypnotised is not made aware of the hypnotic process, this makes it a bit hit and miss as we will see in a later chapter.

Also it raises certain moral questions which we are definitely not discussing in this book. My only advice would be that hypnotists must always have the best interest of the hypnotee in mind.

For the purpose of this book we will be focussing mainly on overt speed hypnosis.

Regular inductions

To really get a grasp of the various processes involved we should take a broad look at the function of hypnosis and the technical aspects.

First let's look at a standard therapeutic hypnosis induction, see how and why it works.

Once we understand this then we can understand what is required to perform speed hypnosis.

I'm going to describe a very common and probably the oldest form of induction.

This is called a Progressive Relaxation Hypnotic Induction it relies on focusing the attention and relaxing the hypnotee both physically and mentally.

After performing some simple suggestibility tests which are described further along in a later chapter the hypnotists asks the hypnotee to sit and get comfortable. Here's how it goes.

Once comfortable they are asked to take several deep breaths, in through their nose and out through mouth. Each time they exhale they are encouraged to let go of bodily tension.

Then they are asked to look at a single spot on the wall or ceiling, or the tip of a pen being held by the hypnotist, anywhere, it really does not matter and keep their attention fixed on that spot.

The spot should be up above the natural eye line. This is why some hypnotists chose a pen or similar object. They are then able to control where the focus is placed.

The hypnotist will then speak in a low slow relaxing tone using a script something like the one on the following pages

. Between each sentence there is a slight pause of about two seconds, just enough time for the hypnotee to absorb the information.

These pauses are indicated by the ellipses.

Keep Looking at that spot...

Don't take your eyes of it for a moment...

Focus all your attention on it...

At the same time listen to my voice...

Follow my instructions...

Continue breathing...

Allow the sounds and smells...

Around you...

To wash across you...

As you listen to my voice...

And focus on that single spot...

Good...

I want you to go inside...

As if you could go inside yourself...

And think about your feet...

I want you to think about your feet...

In particular your toes...

Imagine what it would be like...

To allow the tension to leave your toes...

All the tiny muscles that move your toes...

Let them just relax...

Think about...

What it would be like if those toes were so relaxed...

More relaxed than they've ever been before...

Take a second and allow that to happen...

Allow your toes to become completely relaxed...

That's right...

Completely relaxed and heavy...

Comfortable, heavy and relaxed...

Now take that relaxed feeling...

Take it and let it spread up through your feet too...

That's right...

Gently slowly...

The relaxed feeling covering your feet...

As well as your toes...

Good...

Just take a second and allow that to happen...

The muscles of your feet and toes comfortable...

All tension gone from your toes and feet...

Excellent now feel that feeling of complete relaxation...

That deeply comfortable feeling...

Moving along and up...

Notice it gradually moving...

Moving up into your shins and calves...

Feeling so r-e-l-x-e-d...

As if the muscles weren't working...

From your toes all the way to your knees...

Every muscle completely relaxed...

Still concentrating on that spot...

Still listening to my voice...

Every breath you take and every word I say helps you to...

Just completely and utterly relax those muscles...

Excellent, now feel that feeling moving up to your hips...

Through your upper legs...

Your thighs right the way up...

You can feel that...

Now...

That heavy deeply comfortable relaxation...

Covering your entire lower body...

That's right all tension gone from your hips...

All the way down to your toes...

Sinking down into the chair...

And now notice that relaxed feeling...

That feeling of relaxation flowing up...

Flowing right through your torso...

All the way up through your stomach...

Every muscle relaxes and let's go...

Up through your chest...

And at the same time through your back...

So that now as you breathe you notice...

You notice noticing just how comfortable you are...

So pleasantly comfortable...

Comfortable and relaxed...

Right the way down across your body your legs...

And your toes...

Heavy and relaxed right down...

To your toes...

And just take a moment to experience that heavy...

Comfortable and safe feeling...

And as that comfortable safe feeling takes you over feel it moving...

All the way across your shoulders...

As those shoulders just sink...

Sink down heavy and limp...

Into the chair...

And that limp heavy sensation...

Moving down your arms and into your hands...

And as you breath feel that relaxation continue into every finger...

So that you become so relaxed from your shoulders...

All the way down into your toes...

Now as you breath out feel that relaxation move up across your face...

Over your chin...

Your cheeks...

Your forehead...

And right around the back of your head...

And all the way around your entire head...

Feel this wonderful state take over your whole body...

And as it does...

Feel your eyelids begin to feel heavy and tired...

That's right and as they blink...

And feel heavier and heavier...

Wanting to just close down...

Allow those eyelids to just drop down...

As you yourself drop down into a wonderful state of hypnosis...

Now your entire body is completely relaxed...

Imagine what it will be like to double that relaxation...

As if your whole body from the top of your head to the tips your toes...

Were two times relaxed...

That's good just double that relaxation throughout your body...

Good and one more time allow that relaxed feeling to wash down...

All the way down from the top of your head to the tips of your toes...

Once again doubling...

Taking you as deep as you need to go.

That is a very basic relaxation induction for hypnosis. Here is a simple breakdown of how it works.

We started with the deep breaths, this naturally relaxes the body as we take in a large gulp of air and as we exhale the body sinks thus starting the whole process off.

The mentioning of letting go of tension helping. Also the hypnotee is encouraged to breath out through their mouth. this sends air across the lips which is a natural comforter which in turn helps with sensations of safety.

Next the looking at a spot high up causes eye strain, together narrowing the focus allowing the mind to have a sort of tunnel vision this also has an effect on the voice being received.

The hypnotee gets a sort of tunnel hearing, especially when the hypnotist says things like listen ti my voice.

Then the verbal suggestions of relaxation begins.

What happens here is the hypnotee is literally being sent into a daydream state of mind.

To better understand this let's take a look at how the mind is considered to function is essential.

The mind

There are three parts to the mind.

The conscious

The unconscious

The critical factor.

The conscious is our calculating part of the brain. Its what we consider to be 'ME' it can reason and it thinks logically.

The unconscious is the imagination part of the brain the unconscious also holds memories, beliefs and habits.

Whenever we make decisions, although we would like to think otherwise, it is the unconscious that is at work.

You can test this yourself, when we watch a movie or read a book or hear a story that is spooky or scary, it creates a state of mind which persists after the movie or book or story we go to bed.

As we walk up the stairs our imagination is prone to take over and we often get a sensation that makes us slightly uncomfortable.

This is the unconscious whispering to us, 'watch out it might be real.' It doesn't matter how hard the conscious tells us that ghosts don't exist we can still easily be spooked.

When the hypnotist wants to get a hypnotee to do something it is the unconscious that needs to be communicated with.

The third part, the critical factor is perhaps the most important. This is like a guard standing between the conscious and unconscious. It acts as a filter, so new information doesn't seep into the unconscious to become a new belief or habit.

When information comes into the mind it encounters the guard then the guard refers to the unconscious. The unconscious in turn tells the guard if something is true or false depending on previous experience or beliefs.

Then the guard allows the vetted information into the conscious part of the mind or dispels it.

With the progressive relaxation detailed above. The guard is literally sent to sleep by making him think that the Information is boring. Once he is asleep the new information is easily passed to the unconscious. That's how hypnotherapy works. Once the guard is bypassed we slip a new reality into the unconscious

Well obviously it is more complicated than that but it's a good model to use as a rule of thumb.

Speed Vs Regular hypnosis

So you are wondering what the relationship between speed hypnosis and regular hypnosisis is.

The link, as I'm sure you have figured out, is the critical factor, in the progressive hypnosis we had him narrow his focus to one thing then we sent him off to sleep. Slowly and gradually

With speed hypnosis we need to get around him in other ways. We can use shock or confusion on him, or combination of the two then quickly narrow the focus to keep them in trance.

Shocking the critical factor is probably the most common you have witnessed on TV or at a hypnosis show, the most popular of these is the hand to face hypnosis induction.

It is very similar to what happens to someone when they have a traumatic experience.

The critical factor literally freezes, like at the aftermath of a car crash. The victims are in shock and when a cop or a medical worker speaks to them they simply obey.

The critical factor just doesn't know what to do with itself and so gives up control to the external input.

This is why doctors have to be very careful about how they speak to patients immediately after delivering bad news. Look at these two examples.

A doctor announces to a patient that they have cancer. The patient will almost certainly ask if it is terminal and how long they have left, when they ask this question they are in shock their critical factor is on the floor defeated and their unconscious is like a sponge.

If the doctor replies that he has known others who have survived for years, that there are always new drugs and treatments, and there is always hope this will have a positive effect on the patient.

of course they will have bad days as well as good but the unconscious mind will hang on the words **'hope and years'**.

If however the doctor simply says you have six months. The patient is almost certain to die in six months. The effect of there being no wiggle room is very negative.

The unconscious will only hear the words **'six months'** in fact it will even set up a clock or timetable and the body will run down accordingly.

Let's look at an example of bypassing the critical factor by using a common method. The handshake to hand in front of face method.

The hand to face is very effective. The TV mentalist Derren Brown from the UK uses this technique to great effect, what's more he appears to do it 'cold' that is to say without any priming of the hypnotee.

A great example of this is when he gets a young man to go to his bank and draw out five thousand pounds.

Here's how he does it:

He approaches the guy in the street. He puts his hand out for a handshake, as the guy brings his own hand up to reciprocate Derren grabs the offered hand by the wrist using his free hand. he then pulls the victims hand up in front of his face with the palm facing him, he speaks a few words and the guy is hypnotised.

Then Derren goes on to tell the guy to withdraw the money and come back.

To the audiences amazement the man goes off to the bank and returns with the money.

What Derren did is set up what is known in the business as a 'pattern interrupt'.

When he offers his hand for the handshake the unconscious part of the hypnotees brain automatically brings his Hand up.

Now the guard is not even watching because it's such a usual and mundane thing he doesn't have to alert the unconscious to anything untoward.

When his wrist is grabbed the guard is momentarily shocked and doesn't know what to do, then he is immediately confused by what is going on just as in the car crash. He literally freezes. Then comes the soothing tones of the hypnotist.

So he sort unfreezes and then just slouches in his chair, saying this was all a bit much but now it's OK because the unconscious is having a friendly safe sounding chat.

Once the hand is in front of the face the narrowing focus comes into play. And the unconscious is accessible.

All in all its very elegant and dramatic, there are other factors at work here too, so don't expect you could just go out and perform this on any old passer-by.

Although it appears to be a 'cold' speed induction that isn't strictly true. Read on!

Derren explains to the audience that the guy he just hypnotised has previously applied to be on the show, he just doesn't know when or even if he will be asked to appear or in what capacity. During the pre-screening process he has been evaluated as a highly susceptible personality type.

This means that Derren knows he has a predisposition to being hypnotised.

Another and perhaps more important factor is Derren himself or more to the point his celebrity status and reputation.

When Derren approaches his victim in the street he allows the guy to see him for a second or two. Making sure he is recognised. This creates a sense of excitement and panic in the soon to be hypnotised man.

Simply seeing and recognising Derren puts his guard into a state of mild panic, it's sort of skirting about thinking, 'shit! Something is going to happen its Derren brown the hypnotist I don't know what's going to happen but I know something will.' Of course when the guard consults with the unconscious it is in total agreement.

So when the routine begins the poor guy is ninety percent of the way there. His critical factor has sort of given up already and said to itself I might as well let it happen.

So in fact it is very likely that Derren could have walked up to this guy and simply shouted the word 'SLEEP!' at him and he would have complied.

As I said before although technically it is a cold routine it's not really. It just looks that way.

Confusion

Another type of speed induction uses confusion, this entails giving the critical factor, or 'guard', so many tasks to do at one time that he gives up and slumps in his chair again.

This kind of confusion technique is used very successfully in television advertising.

Pictures are flashed in front of you each lasting about a second. By the time the guard can process one image and reference with the unconscious, another appears, then another then another etc.

After fifteen seconds or so the guard is actually spinning, that's when the soothing or commanding message appears. This message is received by the unconscious without question.

Adverts for vehicles use this technique quite often. they show you a moving car in half a dozen or so different situations, so fast that you only get a sense of the car, you don't really get a good look at it then it will link to other things like pretty women, good times, lots of friendly people, basically you being popular.

Then comes the catch, a long picture of the emblem or badge and a voiceover telling you something like 'life was never before so much fun'.

Incredibly we haven't actually had a good look at the car in detail and yet many will have fallen for it.

If you want to see proof of this phenomena observe someone watching one of these adverts, their faces actually relax so much sometimes their jaws drop and their eyes glaze over, the archetypal trance look.

So if performing a confusion style induction the hypnotist will be looking for this blank expression.

Confusion Induction

When using this principle in a hypnotic induction it might go something like this:

Concentrate on your body...

Notice how your left hand feels heavy...

As your right arm feels light...

At the same time your left leg feels even lighter...

Than your right heavier leg...

And your right hand goes up...

As your left leg wants to go down...

You see where this is going. The hypnotist is saying things which relate to the hands and legs, so it appears on one level to make sense, but is actually nonsensical.

So we have looked at the so called 'cold' inductions, now let's look at a more realistic ways of using speed hypnosis, that is getting the hypnotee primed and ready for hypnosis then use a speed induction. This route brings much more success.

Trying out 'cold' inductions on complete strangers brings about forty to fifty percent success rate.

Whereas following a sensible structure of priming and convincing brings something like ninety five to one hundred percent success.

Realistic speed

First we would start with some tests and convincers.

The first thing to do is to see who is genuinely interested in hypnosis when you announce that you are able to help people become hypnotised.

The more genuine their interest the more likely they will respond to the induction.

You have a part to play in this too be enthusiastic be cheerful and confident, make people want to know more.

Ue the correct positive language and body language and you will have more volunteers and success. Remember the doctor and the cancer patient.

Once you have some interested parties tell them that you can show them some neat tricks.

These 'tricks' are in fact tests but keep that to yourself.

You are using these tricks to identify the eventual target or targets for the actual hypnosis.

Guaranteed tricks

There are several tests/ tricks. Perhaps the most popular is the magnetic finger trick, this is when a hypnotist gets the hypnotee to clamp their fingers together in front of their face

Then they are instructed to unfold both index fingers and point them skywards about an inch apart.

The hypnotee is then told something like this:

Squeeze your other fingers as hard as you can into the...

Backs of your hands...

Now concentrate on the two index fingers...

Imagine that in the tips of your fingers are two magnets...

Two very powerful magnets...

Pulling your fingers towards each other...

Let it happen...

Don't try to stop it...

Don't try to help it...

Just let those fingers move together...

Because those magnets just keep pulling together...

Closer, closer and closer...

The hypnotist carries on like this the fingers will come together, the quicker this happens the more suggestible the person is.

Some hypnotists call this the 'guaranteed magnetic fingers' because, if the hypnotee follows the instructions fully, it is physically impossible for them not to come together.

In fact anyone whose fingers do not come together is making a deliberate effort to keep them apart, do not attempt to hypnotise them they can continue with the tricks but will try to make you look bad later in the demonstration. if you are determined that you want to hypnotise one of these people then do it after you have hypnotised others and only if they have shown signs of waking trance at some point.

Another guaranteed trick is the interlocked hands above the heads, for this the hypnotee stands or sits, they interlace their hands in front of them, with the palms facing in and the fingers straight across the back of the opposite hand.

The hands are then rotated outwards simulating a sort of hand clasp stretching. Then the arms are raised above the head, so that the hypnotee appears to be pushing up.

The hypnotist then says something along the lines of.

Push up as hard as you can...

As if you were trying to push your hands right up through the ceiling...

Keep your elbow locked tight...

Do not let up for a moment...

Push as hard as you can...

That's right up and up...

I'm going to count to five and when I reach the number five...

You will not be able to pull your hands apart...

One push up as high as you can...

Two higher and higher up into the sky....

Three those hands are bonging together...

As if the strongest super glue were bonding them...

Sticking them together like one solid piece...

Four sticking tighter and tighter...

The higher they go the more they stick...

Higher and higher...

And five completely stuck...

So stuck that when you try to pull them apart they stay stuck...

Try...

Try and see they are stuck...

Stuck tight...

And the harder you try the more they stick...

And stop trying...

The hypnotist will typically now step in and take their arms bending them at the elbows telling the hypnotee that all has returned to normal.

Again it is physically impossible for someone to pull their hands apart in this position if they follow the instructions correctly.

Other Tricks

Right so enough of the guaranteed tricks let's look at some that involve more verbal suggestion,

These verbal only tricks can be done after a couple of guaranteed ones. since the volunteers are becoming more convinced you are creating the Derren Brown effect of presupposition, mentioned earlier, in them.

If the potential hypnotee succeeds with these ones this shows genuine suggestibility since to be successfully they are responding purely to suggestion.

The rising arm

The hypnotee will sit in a chair, usually an arm chair. They place their arm on the chair. They can have their eyes open or closed it doesn't matter.

The hypnotist then gets their arm to float up off the arm of the chair by using only the power of suggestion.

There are literally dozens of different routes to take with the verbal suggesting. Below are a couple of examples which can be changed or modified to suit the situation.

For one hypnotist may suggest that a helium balloon is attached to the arm in question.

Another method is to simply suggest the arm is getting lighter.

So method one, the balloon, might go something like this.

Close your eyes...

I want you to picture a very large red balloon...

A large bright light red balloon...

So light that it would float off high into the sky if it were let go...

It won't float away because it is tied to your hand...

It's tied to your wrist by a piece of string...

It wants to float up...

Float up and away...

It's so light it starts to tug gently at the string...

Pulling upwards all the time...

Its pulling so much its as if it starts to tug at your wrist...

The big bright light red balloon floating up...

Pulling upwards...

Notice how it pulls your hand up...

Up, up, up all the way...

Higher and higher as the balloon floats...

Floats up towards the sky...

Higher and higher...

Good and your arm goes up and up...

Up with the big red balloon.

Once the arm starts to move the hypnotist will feed back his observations as suggestions. Compounding the effect.

Yes that's right...

As you feel that arm going...

Up, up and up...

Still further the higher it goes the higher it can go...

After not very long the arm will be a considerable way off the arm

Another good suggestibility only test is the light heavy arms if this is performed directly after the floating arm success likely hood of success is improved immensely.

The hypnotee is seated and the hypnotist suggests that one arm is floating up and the other moving down something like this:

Hold your arms out in front of you...

At shoulder height...

Good...

Now close your eyes...

Have your right hand palm facing down...

And your left hand palm facing up...

In a moment I'm going to gently tap your right hand...

(Tap) like this...

When I do I want you to imagine that your hand...

Your right hand is getting lighter...

(Tap) lighter and lighter with each word I say and each breath you take...

And when I tap your left hand...

(Tap) like this...

It will feel as if it is getting heavier...

And heavier...

Right arm light and rising (tap)...

Left arm sinking down and heavy (tap)...

Right arm lighter than air...

As light as a helium balloon...

Left arm feeling like at has a heavy leather bound library book in it...

Heavier and heavier...

As I place another book on it (tap)

And that right bright light hand goes steadily up higher and higher..

Noticing how nice that feels to just let it happen

That left arm going down while the right arm goes up

Because the heavier that left arm gete

The lighter the right hand becomes.

the hypnotists continues with these instructions until a gap is evident between the height of the hands.

Then he will get them to open their eyes and see how much distance there is. this is not only a good convincer for the hypnotees but also the hypnotist will once again be able to gauge how well individuals will respond to the speed induction when the time comes.

The more distance the better the potential.

These tricks have several effects on the hypnotee. It shows the hypnotee that things do happen when the hypnotists says so.

It creates the awe that we mentioned earlier. So presupposition takes over the mind. They are in a position where they assume that hypnosis will happen.

Another thing is that it creates trust or rapport between the two. Without trust the critical factor ' guard' will be on high alert making it very hard to get him to sleep or distracted.

A really good way to establish trust awe expectation is the sway test.

Sway Test

The hypnotee is asked to stand up. The hypnotist then pushes their feet together and stands behind them.

He rocks them around and tell them that they have to trust him implicitly. He keeps his hand on their shoulders and holds them up straight.

The hypnotee at this point may or may not trust the hypnotist. That will soon change!

The hypnotist lets go of the hypnotee having unbalanced them. Then they say something like this:

In a moment I m going to get you to close your eyes.

Once your eyes are closed you will feel yourself falling backwards.

There is nothing to worry about

I will not let you fall

The hypnotist now takes his hands away. And continues.

OK now close your eyes

And feel yourself falling backwards into my arms.

That's right. I won't let you fall.

Moving, swaying falling all the way back.

At this point the hypnotee will fall back and usually stop themselves by stepping back.

The hypnotist stands them back up and says.

Let yourself go.

Allow yourself to fall into me.

That's right I will catch you.

This is repeated until the hypnotee is falling back with complete trust.

Now the hypnotist moves around to the front and repeats the exercise several times. Until the hypnotee is falling with ease in any direction and the hypnotist is 'saving' them.

Inductions

The hypnotist has now helped the hypnotee to accept that what he suggests will happen. And that he can be trusted to catch them.

Once at this stage the hypnotist will move onto a rapid induction. The one below is an ideal one to use after the magnetic fingers.

The hypnotist now sits the hypnotee down. Lifted their arms in front of them and holds them straight out about shoulder width apart. Palms facing inwards towards each other.. The hypnotist then continues like so.

In a moment not quite yet...

Your hands are going to be magnetised together...

As I speak you will notice that they start to move together...

Just like when you feel backwards...

You do not have to make it happen...

Just let it happen...

Don't try to stop it ether. Just let those hands come slowly together...

OK start to feel those hands moving towards each other...

You don't even have to listen to what I am saying...

My voice will go with you...

You notice that they move towards each other...

And as they start to move together you can allow yourself to notice how your eyes become heavier...

And heavier...

And its as if the closer your hands get together the heavier and heavier those eyelids become...

That's right closer and closer...

Heavier and heavier...

Feeling more and more comfortable as those hands come together...

Like a magnet pulling them towards each other...

And your eyes get heavier and heavier...

Usually after a minute or so the arms have moved about halfway towards each other. And the hypnotees eyes will be fluttering.

The hypnotist continues with the suggestions adding some extra statements.

Your hands get closer...

And eventually when those hands touch...

Your eyes will close and you will relax into hypnosis...

Closer and closer...

Heavier and heavier...

When the hands are about four to six inches apart. The hypnotist will push them together very quickly and pull them down and forwards slightly commanding sleep.

The hypnotee will crash down into a deep stated of hypnosis there and then.

You see it's a clever mixture of lulling the guard into a false sense of security by having the hypnotee do the mundane task of the hands coming together.

He will be a bit fascinated too because it will appear to be happening by itself.

He is also narrowed his focus to one single thought.

The connection is then made between the hands getting closer and the eyes closing. Then at the prescribed time shock is used by pulling the hands and commanding sleep.

The whole thing should take less than two minutes. With this type of speed induction the critical factor doesn't stand a chance.

Another good induction which is used typically after the sway trick is the falling back induction.

The hypnotist will continue from the sway test and after catching the hypnotee several times will allow them to drop, still catching them but instead of stopping them from almost upright they won't catch until the hypnotee is almost horizontal.

This shocks the critical factor as they drop a lot further than they have become accustomed to in the trick.

As they are caught the gaurd sighes in relief, of course the hypnotisist continues to sooth.

Deeper

An important thing at this point is deepening. Remember the progressive relaxation induction. The critical factor was bored to sleep. So he will happily snooze for quite a while.

When you use speed induction he was startled. If nothing is done he will immediately come back.

In fact many inexperienced hypnotists who try speed don't think that it worked because they don't continue talking and the hypnotee comes around.

Deepeners do exactly what they suggest. They take the hypnotee more deeply into trance.

So as soon as the hypnotists commands sleep at the end of a speed induction he will continue along these lines.

Just allow that wonderful feeling wash across your body...

Deeper and deeper with every word I say...

Feeling every muscle in your body relax...

Deeper and deeper...

Allowing yourself to just let go...

Lots of hypnotist will gently rock the hypnotees head at the same time. This is said to aid in the physical sensation of relaxing.

Once this is done the hypnotist will usually carry out what is known as a structured deepened like so.

You are standing at the top of a winding staircase...

The staircase is well lit...

And there is a sturdy handrail...

In a moment you are going Togo down the stairs...

With each step you find you relax more...

Move forward and step on to the first step...

Down onto the first step deeper and deeper...

Good that's it...
And on down to the next step...

Two as you feel yourself go two times deeper...

Down feeling more comfortably relaxed as you step forward...

And step down to the third step as you notice you go three times deeper again...

Feeling that blanket of relaxation wrapping around you...

As you take the next step down onto step number four just takes you...

Four times deeper still...

Deeper and deeper so relaxed now...

And because you go down to five...

It's as if you go five times down further deeper more comfortable...

The deeper you go the better you feel and the better you feel the deeper you go...
Go now to the next step...

Step number six. And as you step onto that next step...

You feel yourself go six times deeper still...

Deeper down into the depths of that wonderful relaxed state...

Because feeling this relaxed is so comfortable...

You just go down onto the next step easily and softly...

Step seven as you feel yourself going seven times deeper...

Deeper and deeper eight as you take that next step..

And nine times deeper you go down onto step number nine...

Now down again as you step down to that final step...

And feel yourself going ten times deeper...

And standing on that last step you can see the basement of relaxation...

In front of you and your foot goes forward and off that last step...

Onto the basement floor as you feel that feeling of being....

Completely and utterly relaxed...

These deepeners can take many forms. The trick is that the hypnotist encourages a downward motion linked to deepening of the hypnosis.

Now the hypnotist has choices. Depending on why he has hypnotised the hypnotee in the first place.

If it is being done for fun. For example the hypnotist has used a speed induction in a pub in order to entertain a group of friends. Under these circumstances the hypnotee will be performing silly activities.

With each successive action carried out by the hypnotee they will become more suggestible. This is one of the great things about the hypnotic state.

Phenomena

The hypnotist brings the arm of the hypnotee up in front of him at shoulder height.

He then taps at various places along the arm. The shoulder the elbow and wrist most commonly. As he gives the verbal suggestions.

Imagine your arm is becoming stiff...

Stiff and straight...

Like a solid piece of wood...

The shoulder is locked (tap)...

The elbow is locked (tap)...

The wrist is locked...

The whole arm becoming completely rigid...

Stiffer and stiffer with each second...

More rigid as if it were made from a single, solid, block

of wood...

Completely solid...

so solid that if you try to move it...

It just stays there...

The harder you try to move your arm the harder it is...

If I push it...

It just stays there...

It bounces right back...

Solid, rigid, stiffer and stiffer...

The hypnotist will test to make sure that full arm rigidity

Excellent now in a moment when I count to three...

You will find that your arm has returned to normal...

It will become completely loose and limp...

One two three

The hypnotist will take the hypnotee by the wrist and keep the now limp arm in the air.

When I drop that arm and it lands heavily in your lap you will find you go even deeper relaxed

The downward movement of the arm coupled with the verbal suggestion takes the hypnotee deeper into trance.

Another fun phenomena that is a handy convincer and entertaining as hell is the foot stick.

The hypnotist simply makes suggestion that the hypnotees foot is stuck to the ground.

As you sit there and relax more and more with each breath...

I want you to focus now on your left foot.

And as you focus you notice that it is feeling heavier...

So heavy in fact that it's hard to move it...

And because it's so heavy it's as if it's becoming stuck...

Like its becoming stuck by the world's strongest super glue

To the floor

Sticking tight

Locking

Sinking...

Bonding...

Gluing...

To the floor...

It's so firmly stuck that if you try to lift it...

It gets more stuck...

It becomes so stuck that the harder you try...

The harder it is to lift it...

The harder you try...

The harder it is...

Try and find that its stuck fast...

OK stop trying and notice now how that stuck feeling moves from your foot...

The hypnotist takes the hypnotees arm and places it on their head.

Notice that that stuck feeling is now in your hand...

And it sticks to your head...

I can take it off with ease...

The hypnotist lifts the hand off and replaces it...

You see I can take it off but when I put it back...

It's as if it sticks a thousand times stronger...

Each time I take it off and put it back it just sticks even harder...

The hypnotist will remove and re-stick the hand several times...

By this time the hypnotee will perform just about any comic suggestion the hypnotist gives them...

Emergence

Once the hypnotist has finished his demonstration he will then wake up the hypnotee.

A lot of emphasis is put on this in literature. However even though it is quite a simple process it must be done properly.

The most important thing here is that the hypnotist removes all traces of suggestions made during the hypnosis.

It will go something like this.

In a moment I'm going to count up to five...

By the time I reach the number five you will be wide awake...

With all suggestions gone...

You will be back to normal...

One feeling yourself becoming more alert...

Two eyes becoming more active...

Three felling energy com in back into your body...

Four that's right your whole body becoming more alive and alert...

Five eyes open wide awake completely alert now...

That is the simplest and quickest awakening there is.

Lots of hypnotist will build in the hypnotic gift and the instant hypnosis trigger. To do this they add extra suggestions into the awakening like so:

In a moment I'm going to wake you up...

I will count to five and when I reach five you will be wide awake...

Wide awake and back in the here and now...

So one...

Going deeper and deeper all current suggestions gone Two...

Knowing that any time in the future whenever I click my fingers...

You will return to this deeply relaxed place...

It could be in a few minutes or even next week...

It could be next month or even ten years from now...

Whenever you see me click my fingers you will return to trance...

Three...Starting to wake up feeling confident...

Ready to carry on with your day...

Feeling like you have had a five hour massage...

And an eight hour sleep...

Feeling completely refreshed...

Four...Energy returning to your body eyes beginning to flutter and open...

And five...Eyes open now and completely wide awake...

Thanks for reading this book. Please take a moment to visit the site that you ordered it from and leave a review.